My First Piano Book

Learning The Musical Alphabet Through Stories

Book Three

Written and Illustrated by Katrin Arefy, creator of *The Golden Key to Piano* teaching method and founder of Golden Key Piano School in Berkeley California.

My First Piano Book

My First Piano Book. Copyright © 2010 by Golden Key Piano School Inc., Publishing Department. All rights reserved. No parts of this book may be used or reproduced in any manner whatsoever without written permission. For information address Golden Key Piano School Publishing Department. 1809 University Ave, Berkeley CA, 94703

www.goldenkeypianoschool.com

My First Music Book is a series of interactive teaching tools designed to be used in group music classes for children 3 to 5 years of age. This foundation course engages and prepares young students for further private piano lessons providing the necessary education for young students before sitting down at the piano.

The attractive stories in this book foster students' imaginations and readily stick in their minds. This easy and fun process gives young students a strong foundation to be used throughout their education in music.

Using these books children will learn:

- The musical alphabet
- The note values
- The musical staff
- The basics of the keyboard
- The dynamics

This book can be also used as a self study tool for learning the musical alphabet at home with help of a parent.

Visit us online at www.thegoldenkeytopiano.com to watch demo videos, view other music books, or ask questions.

About teaching this book in a group class

Each class is half an hour long and includes sing-along children songs, listening and repeating tonal and rhythm patterns, listening to the teacher play a few age appropriate songs on the piano (see *A Thousand Stories for a Little Pianist*), playing matching games on the white board, playing along with musical instruments such as egg shakers and cymbals and, of course, story time.

The stories in *My First Piano Book* are used in story time to teach one symbol or musical alphabet in each class. Reviewing the symbols over and over in class will help the students remember them forever.

Accent

This sign sits above or below a note and tells you to play or sing that note louder than others. It is called an *Accent*.

1. Try to draw an accent for these notes.

2. Clap these notes and count for each one. Clap the ones with accent louder.

$\frac{2}{4}$ *Time Signature*

Listen to your teacher play this march:

Animal's March

Kattrin Arefy

Stand up and march along with the music, counting for each step: **one**, two, **one**, two.

The $\frac{2}{4}$ time signature sounds like a march.
One, two, **one,** two, **heavy**, light, **heavy**, light.

Clap these notes. Is it $\frac{2}{4}$ music?

Try to write the $\frac{2}{4}$ time signature at the beginning of the line.

A Story of a Sunny Day, Marching in the Park

One sunny day, you quarter note and seven other of your friends, who are also quarter notes, got together to go out to the park. One daddy half note was also with you. You all marched to the park happily counting: one, two, one, two. Queen G happened to be looking outside her castle's window and she saw you marching.

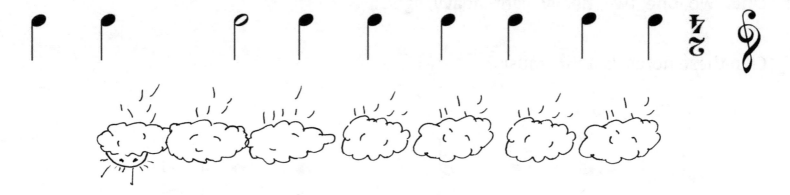

As soon as you got to the park and started to play, the clouds covered the sun. And soon after that...

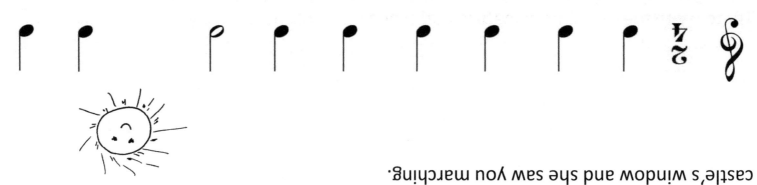

It started to rain. You quarter note, all your friend quarter notes, and daddy half note were getting wet and cold. At this moment, Queen G saw this and decided to help you. She ordered some walls to be built in the park so that all of you could go in the rooms and stay dry.

Since you were marching to the park, Queen G set the rules so that there should be two counts in each room: One, two, one, two…or, one and, two and, one and, two and.

Here are the first two walls. Try finishing the walls by putting two counts in each room.

Reviewing the Notes on the Staff

Do you remember Queen G on the second line and King F on the fourth line? Find them and color them green and purple.

Find soldier middle C on his special little line and color him orange.

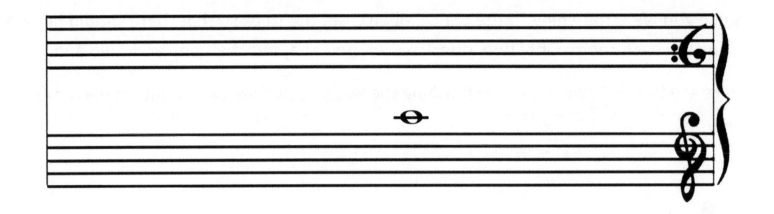

E, the Yellow Elephant in Queen G's Country

Soldier Middle C is not lonely; he has some friends in Queen G's country. Today, you will meet one of his friends. On the first line in Queen G's country lives a yellow elephant. Its name is E, just like Garden E. E is a line note.

Find E on the first line in Queen G's country and color it yellow

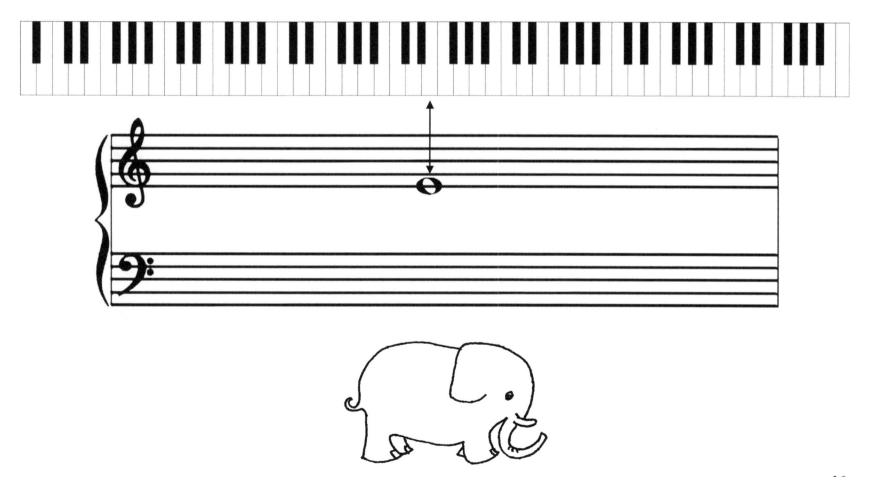

11

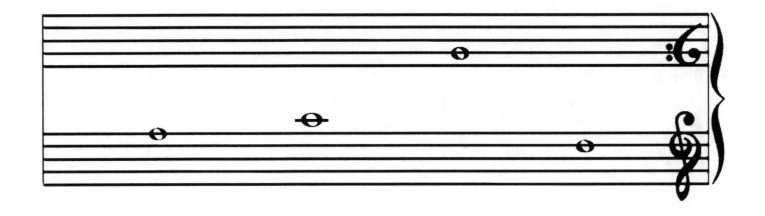

Can you find the other notes and color them with their colors here?

3/4 *Time Signature*

Listen to your teacher play this dance.

Step or clap along with the music counting for each step: **one,** two, three, **one,** two, three.

3/4 time signature sounds like a dance. **One**, two, three, **one**, two, three, **heavy**, light, light, **heavy**, light, light.

Clap these notes. Is it 3/4 music?

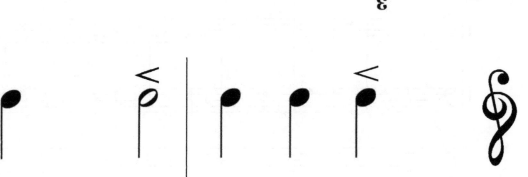

Try to write the 3/4 time signature at the beginning of the line.

A Story of a Sunny Day, Dancing in the Park

One sunny day you quarter note and eleven other of your friends, who are also quarter notes, got together to go out to the park. One mommy dotted half note was also with you. You all danced to the park, happily counting: one, two, three, one, two, three. Queen G happened to be looking outside her castle's window and she saw you dancing.

As soon as you got to the park and started to play, the clouds covered the sun.

And soon after that...

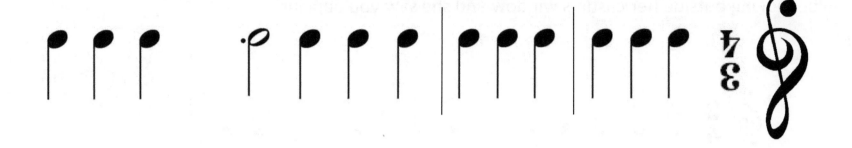

It started to rain. You quarter note, all your friend quarter notes, and mommy dotted half note were getting wet and cold. At this moment, Queen G saw this and decided to help you. She ordered some walls to be built in the park so that all of you could go in the rooms and stay dry.

Since you were dancing to the park, Queen G set the rules so that there should be three counts in each room. One, two, three. Or one and two and three and.

Here are the first two walls. Try finishing the walls by putting three counts in each room.

F, the Purple Clown in Queen G's Country

On the first space of Queen G's country lives a clown. His name is F, just like Garden F, and he always wears purple costume. F is a space note.

Find F on the first space of Queen G's country and color him purple.

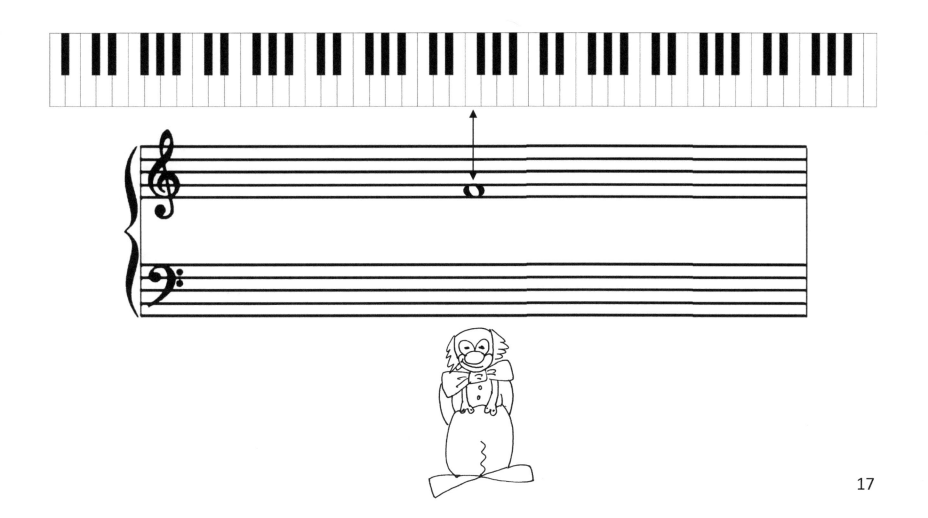

17

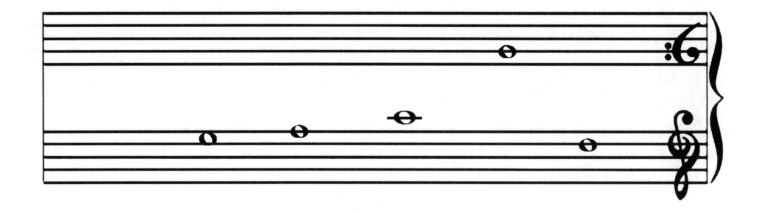

Can you find the other notes and color them with their colors here?

Time Signature 4/4

Listen to your teacher play this lullaby.

Lullaby

Samin Baaghchebaan
Arr. Katrin Arefy

Clap along with the music counting for each step: **one**, two, three, four, **one**, two, three, four.

This is 4/4 time signature. One, two, three, four, one, two, three, four, **heavy**, light, **heavy**, light.

Clap these notes. Is it 4/4 music?

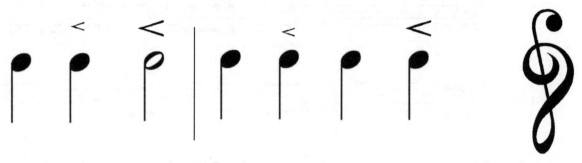

Try to write the 4/4 time signature at the beginning of the line.

A Story of a Sunny Day, Sleeping in the Park

One sunny day you quarter note and eleven other of your friends, who are also quarter notes, got together to go out to the park. Grandma whole note was also with you. You walked to the park, happily counting: one, two, three, four, one, two, three, four. Queen G happened to be looking outside her castle's window and she saw you walking.

When you got to the park you were so tired wanted to take a nap to grandma's lullaby.

But soon...

21

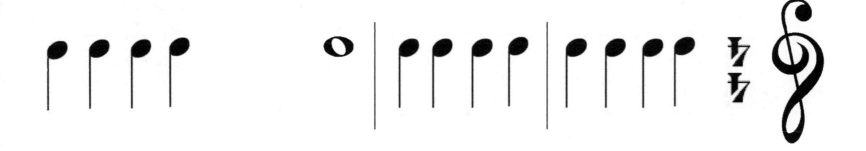

It started to rain. You quarter note, all your friend quarter notes, and grandma whole note were getting wet and cold. At this moment, Queen G saw this and decided to help you. She ordered some walls to be built in the park so that all of you could go in the rooms and sleep.

Since you were walking to the park, Queen G set the rules so that there should be four counts in each room. One, two, three, four. Or, one and two and three and four and.

Here are the first two walls. Try finishing the walls by putting four counts in each room.

D, the Cherry in Queen G's Country

Below the first line of Queen G's country lives a cherry. This cherry has a special name; its name is D, just like Garden D.

Find D below the first line of Queen G's country and color it red.

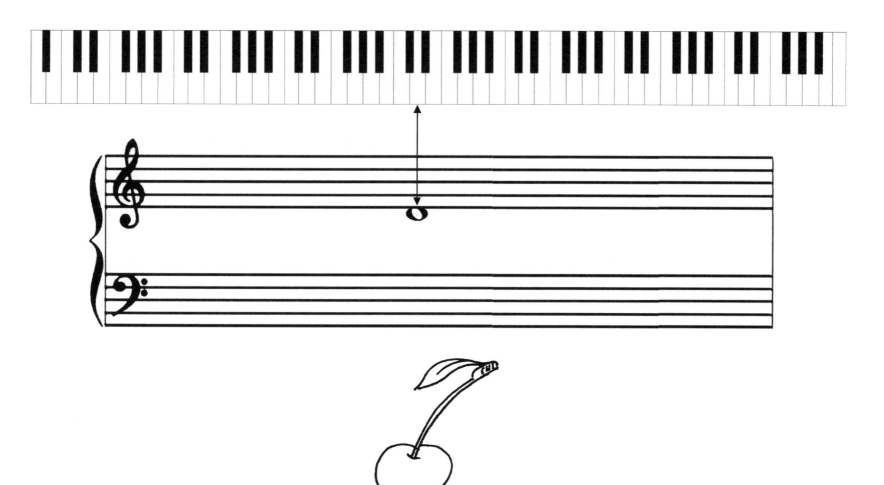

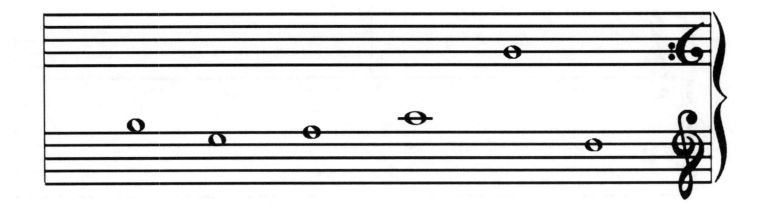

Can you find other notes and color them with their colors here?

Diminuendo

This is a sign that shows you to sing or play gradually softer, and softer, and softer.
It is called a *diminuendo*.

1. Try to draw a *diminuendo* sign.
2. Sing a song first loudly (*forte*) and then sing softer, little by little, so that you finish it softly (*piano*).

A, the Blue Fairy in King F's Country

Soldier Middle C also has some friends in King F's country. There is a blue fairy that lives on the fifth line of King F's country. Her name is A, just like the garden A. She has blue wings.

Find A on the fifth line of King F's country and color her blue.

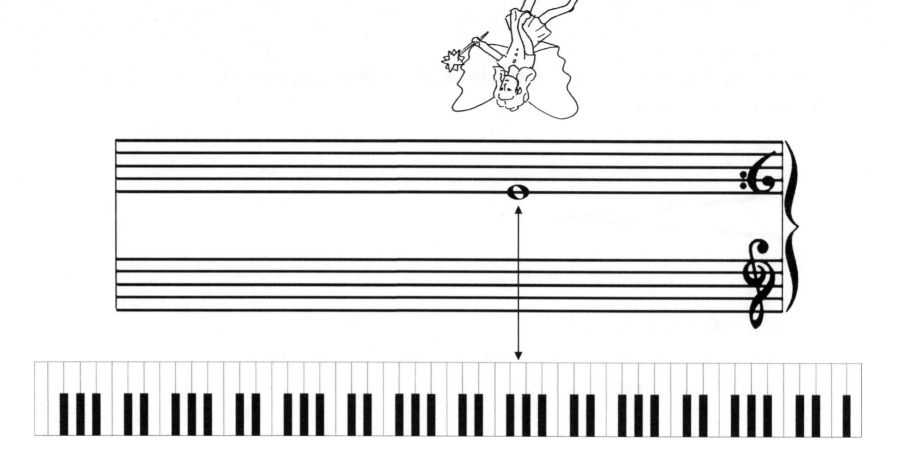

Can you find the other notes and color them with their colors here?

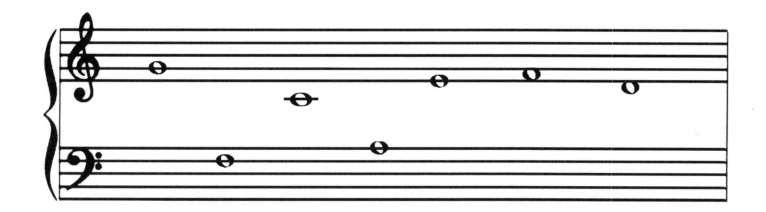

Two Kitty Cats and More

When there is one kitty cat eighth note,
it looks like this:

Take your hands and clap: 1

When there are two kitty cat eighth notes,
they tie their tails together like this:

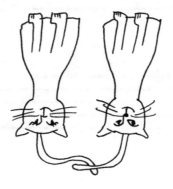

For the first cat we count "1," for the second cat "and." Take your hands and clap for these two kitty cat eighth notes: 1 and

How many kitty cat eighth notes can you find here?

G, the Parrot in King F's Country

There is a green parrot that lives on the fourth line of King F's country. Its name is G, just like Garden G.

Find G on the fourth space of King F's country and color it green.

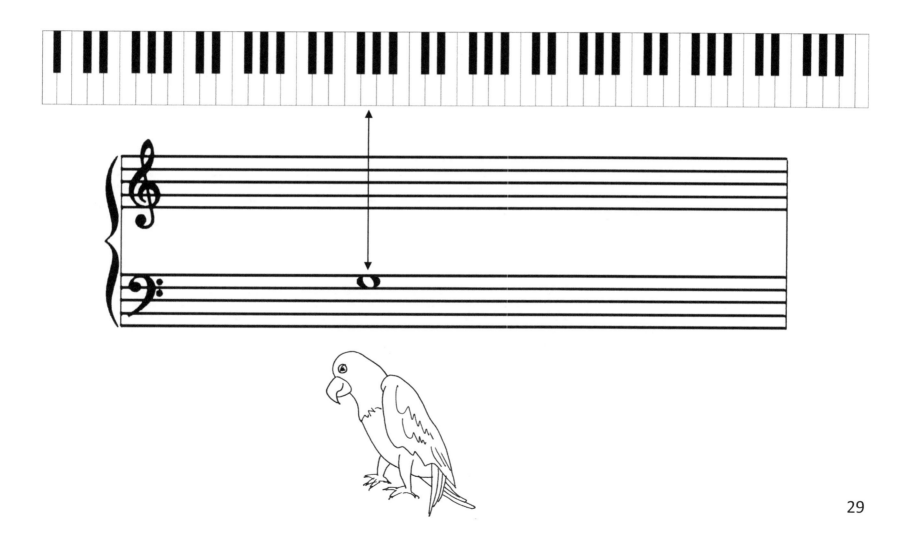

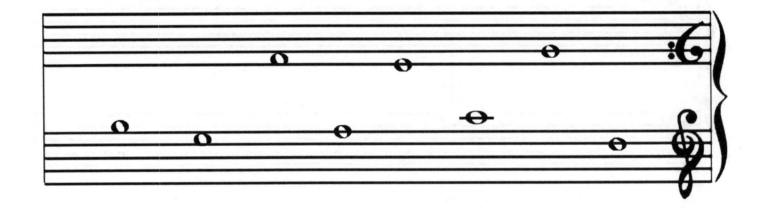

Can you find the other notes and color them with their colors here?

B, the Pony in King F's Country

There is a brown pony that lives above the fifth line of King F's country. Its name is B, just like Garden B.

Find B above the fifth line of King F's country and color it brown.

31

Can you find the other notes and color them with their colors here?

Matching Game: Reviewing the Notes

Match each note with its picture. Color all the notes and the pictures.

www.ingramcontent.com/pod-product-compliance
Lightning Source LLC
LaVergne TN
LVHW061314190225
804088LV00015B/1141